ANIMAL TRACKERS

BY LAKES
&
RIVERS

Tessa Paul

CRABTREE
Publishing Company

CRABTREE
Publishing Company

350 Fifth Avenue
Suite 3308
New York, NY 10118

360 York Road, R.R.4
Niagara-on-the-Lake
Ontario L0S 1J0

73 Lime Walk
Headington, Oxford
England OX3 7AD

Editor **Bobbie Kalman**
Assistant Editor **Virginia Mainprize**
Designers **Emma Humphreys-Davies Richard Shiner Melissa Stokes**

Illustrations by

Front cover: Joanne Cowne; Introduction: Richard Phipps, Rod Sutterby, Jill Wood; Robin Bouttell/WLAA (p.10 – 11), John Cox/WLAA (p.18 –19, 24 – 25), Andrew Becket (p.26), Ruth Grewcock (p.6, 12 – 13), John Morris/WLAA (p.22 – 23), Richard Phipps (p.17), Nick Pike/WLAA (p.16 – 17), Kim Thompson (p.8, 12, 24, 28 – 29, 30 – 31), Guy Troughton/WLAA (26 – 27), Simon Turvey/WLAA (6 – 7, 8 – 9, 16), Jill Wood (p.20 – 21), Mike Woods (p.14 – 15); all track marks by Andrew Beckett

First printed 1997
Copyright © 1997 Marshall Cavendish Ltd.

Cataloging-in-Publication Data

Paul, Tessa
By lakes and rivers / Tessa Paul
p. cm. – – (Animal Trackers)
Includes index.
Summary: Illustrates and describes the tracks of beavers, herons, frogs, and other wetland creatures, with information on the sounds they make, their pawprints and their dwellings.
ISBN 0-86505-586-6 (RLB)   ISBN 0-86505-594-7 (paper)
1. Wetland animals – – Juvenile literature.
2. Animal tracks – – Juvenile literature.
3. Trout – – Juvenile literature
4. Salmon – – Juvenile literature
[1. Wetland animals. 2. Animal tracks.]
I. Title.   II. Series: Paul, Tessa . Animal trackers .
QL113.8. P38   1997......591.768– – dc21   96-49684   CIP AC

Printed and bound in Malaysia

17.95

CONTENTS

INTRODUCTION

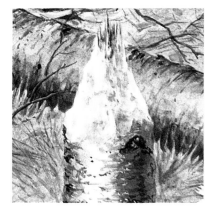

A lake may look still. A river may flow quietly. But if you watch and listen carefully, you will find many animal signs. What are those tunnels in the bank? What is that noise in the air? What is that splash in the water?

There are many animals that live on or near water. Some, such as fish, never leave it. Others stay close to 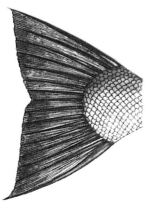 the water's edge. The otter lives on river banks and splashes in the water. Swans nest on the shore. Salmon leap up waterfalls.

Beavers dam up streams to make deep ponds for their homes. Tiny voles dig their tunnels in the dark, damp earth. Close to the shore, herons stand like statues, watching for fish.

This book tells you how to find the creatures that live on or near water. Detailed drawings show you their nests and dens. You will learn the songs the water birds sing. You will find out which animals dig in river banks or live under the roots of trees. You will discover the secret lives of water animals.

OTTER

SLIPPERY PATH
Otters love sliding down slopes on their tummy. Look for slides in the snow or along muddy river banks.

Otters live near water in the empty burrows of other animals. They line their den with wood chips and leaves. Each spring, two or three babies are born. As soon as they grow their waterproof coats, mother teaches her babies to swim. You may see trails leading to the water.

WATER LEGS
The otter's short, powerful legs and webbed toes make it an excellent swimmer. The otter is clumsy on land.

BEAVER

At a narrow part of a river or stream, beavers build their dam. This wall of sticks, roots, and stones blocks the water which then floods into a large pond. In the middle of the pond, beavers build their home, called a lodge.

LAND MARKS
Beavers build mud pies along their trails. They mark these with castorum, their strong-smelling oil. You will see foot prints in the mud.

INSIDE THE LODGE
Living space above the water is dry and cosy. Two tunnels lead down into the water.

POWER GRIP
Beavers can swim while carrying big branches. They hold the stem behind their front teeth.

A STRONG HOME
The lodge is so strong that beaver families live there for many years.

9

The beaver is a born lumberjack. It cuts down tree trunks fifteen inches across. Its long, strong, front teeth are perfect tools for chipping away wood. Beavers cut down trees because they use the wood to build or repair their dam or lodge. Also, they eat tree bark. They store branches under water for winter food.

FIBER DIET
Although they eat mostly trees, beavers also enjoy pond plants such as water lilies. They use their front paws to hold their food. Their big back feet and tail balance them as they sit up to eat.

PAW PRINTS
The front paws have long fingers and thin claws. They are for holding, digging, and building. When swimming, the beaver uses its back, webbed feet as paddles.

TAIL SPLASH

To warn their family of danger, beavers whack their large, flat tail on the water. Then, they dive below the surface. You can hear the loud smack from far away.

FROG

PLANT COLOR
The skin is marked with brown, yellow, and gray. This is good camouflage. Frogs blend in with water plants and are hard to see.

If you sit still and watch a pond, you may see or hear a small splash. It is a frog diving from the shore. You can spot it swimming quickly below the water. In the spring, listen for frog calls. Some frogs chirp like birds, others croak deeply.

SHADY RESTS
Frogs like cool, damp places. They live under shady leaves or in long grass. Sometimes, they sit on water lily leaves in the pond.

TADPOLES
In spring, you may see thick jelly floating in a pond. These frogs' eggs turn into tadpoles. They are round creatures, without arms or legs, and with a long tail. They grow into adult frogs.

WET AND DRY
Frogs are amphibians. They can live in water and on land, but they cannot breathe under water. Frogs have long tongues that flick out and trap slugs, worms, flies, and beetles.

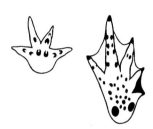

WATERY USES
Webbed feet make the frog a strong swimmer.

MINK

Except during the mating season, mink live alone. The mother and her young stay together for about four months. She teaches them to hunt. Then, they must look after themselves. The males are bigger and more powerful than the females. All mink have a thick, heavy fur coat. It keeps them dry under water and protects them from the cold.

HELPLESS
At birth, baby mink, called kits, are deaf and blind. They are covered with white hair. After six weeks, they leave the den.

NOT CHOOSY
Mink nest in hollow logs or under tree roots. They may take over another animal's empty nest. The mother alone looks after the young mink kits.

HUNTING AND FISHING

Creeping quietly through the grass, mink catch voles, frogs, rabbits, and snakes. They catch fish by herding them into shallow water.

GOOD PICKINGS

Mink stay where the hunting is good. They choose strips of land along a river or marsh. Mostly, they hunt at night.

Mink are excellent hunters. They are quiet and fast and can kill a scurrying vole in a split second. They catch fish, crabs, and crayfish in shallow waters. With a sudden snatch of a paw, they grab their prey. Other, bigger animals hunt mink. They have to watch for coyotes, wolves, bears, and owls.

STRANGE TRAILS
The back feet are partly webbed. The drag of their bushy tail also marks the trail.

PLAYTIME
Baby mink love to play. They hide and pounce. They wrestle on the ground or dive and roll about in the water.

WARNINGS
Mink have a strong smell which warns other animals to keep away.

UNDER WATER
Mink are good swimmers, but they do not see well under water.

TROUT

There are many different kinds of trout. Some are small; others may weigh up to forty pounds. They have spots on their bodies and may have red marks on their bellies. Some live in rivers and streams. Others hide in cool, deep lakes.

WATER SHADES
The color of the trout changes to match light or dark water. This camouflage helps the fish to hide from its predators. It also helps them as they search for prey.

MAYFLY
Trout eat mayfly in early spring. You can see these insects hovering over the river. Watch carefully and you might see a trout gobble a mayfly.

CADDIS FLY
Sometimes, trout lie just below the surface of the water. They suck down insects such as caddis flies. Trout also jump out of the water to catch these and other insects.

19

Trout can stay still for a long time, hiding in the shadows. They move quickly if they see an insect on the water surface. Some trout choose a length of river as their own. As adults, they fight off other fish which try to move into that territory.

MOVING HOUSE
In winter, trout move from their own stretch of river. They look for stony, shallow places where they can spawn, or lay their eggs.

SAFE WATERS
Mink, herons, and otters catch trout in still rivers and shallow streams. It is more difficult to catch trout in fast-moving water.

A SIXTH SENSE

The colored line along the side of a trout's body helps it sense danger. Trout can feel movement in the water.

HATCHERIES

In winter, look in shallow river waters. Trout eggs hatch among stones and in gravel pools. The tiny babies soon swim away to join the adults. When they grow up, trout return to the place where they were born to lay their own eggs.

HERON

Herons live near and in rivers and ponds, but they do not swim. They wade in shallow water near the shore. They use their long bills to spear and snap up fish, frogs, and water snakes. When these birds are frightened, they squawk and croak.

NECK STRETCHES
By watching its neck, you can tell a heron's mood. When angry, it stretches it straight forward. When it is courting, it curves and stretches its neck.

LAND MARKS
The toes are long and thin. Herons wade in water on their stilt-like legs.

SLOW FISHING

Herons stand very still, staring into the water. When a frog or fish comes close, the heron plunges its bill into the water and catches its prey. The bird swallows its meal in one gulp.

BIRD APARTMENTS

Herons nest in colonies. They build large nests of sticks, close together in bushes and trees. They lay about four greenish-blue eggs in spring.

VOLE

Some voles make their homes along rivers and streams. They are strong swimmers and divers. Along the banks, they build long burrows with many entrances. You can see paths of flattened grass between these holes.

GENTLE PAWS
The toes are long, and only part of the paw leaves a print.

HOME IS BEST
Voles line their dens with shredded grass and leaves. They carry food into their burrows and store it in tunnels. The grass outside dens is nibbled short like a lawn.

LITTLE NIBBLES
Voles nibble the new shoots of trees. They strip off bark and chew into tree trunks. You may see their tiny, neat toothmarks.

MESSY DINERS
Voles have favorite eating stones where they carry their food and eat. Look for chewed bits of plants around a stone.

SWAN

All swans live on or near the water. You can see mute swans floating on ponds and lakes in city parks. They are quiet birds but will hiss as a warning. Their wings make a loud, whirring noise when they fly. Whistling swans, also called wild swans, live in the far north of Canada. Each autumn, they migrate south. You can hear their hooting call high in the sky.

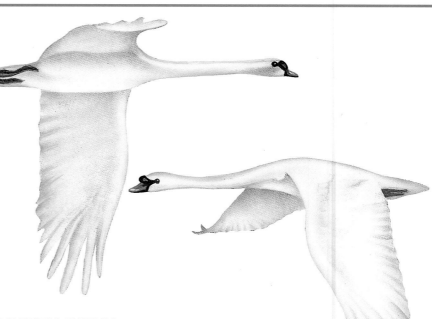

MIGHTY WINGS

Hundreds of whistling swans fly together when they migrate. Look for these huge flocks as they travel each spring. They fly in long, straight lines.

CHANGING LOOKS

The face and the color of the mute swan change as the bird grows older. Young swans have gray feathers and a pale pink bill. They have no knob on their forehead. However, in time, their feathers turn pure white, and their bill becomes orange with a black base. They grow a black knob on their head.

WATER WEBS

This water bird has webbed feet. It can walk on land but does not go far from the shore.

GROUND LEVEL

Swans build nests of moss and grass on the ground. In the cool north, the whistling swan covers her eggs with moss whenever she leaves the nest.

27

LOON

On a still night, you may hear a strange wail echoing across a lake. It is the cry of the loon. Loons also laugh and yodel. They summer on northern lakes. In winter, they migrate to the coast.

WAY BACK
The loon's feet are far back on its body.

GREETINGS
When excited or greeting each other, loons rise out of the water and stretch their neck. Then, they flap their wings.

WINTER CLOTHES
The loon changes color with the seasons. In summer, it has a black head and neck, with a white collar. In winter, its back and neck are gray. The shiny, black bill becomes dull.

DEEP DOWN
Loons can dive 200 feet, chasing fish under water.

A PILE-UP
The nest is a little hollow in the ground or a pile of grass and leaves. Loons lay two green-brown eggs. The chicks hatch after twenty-four days.

SALMON

Salmon change color whenever they make changes in their life. When they move from the sea to rivers, they are green, gray, and blue. After living in the river for a while, they become brown and dark gold, with red spots. Then, salmon lay their eggs and turn dark brown.

TAIL ENDS
It is easy to confuse large trout and salmon. Looking at the tail will help you. The trout's tail fin ends in a straight line. The salmon's fin has a gentle, curved line.

TWO HOMES
Young salmon are born in rivers. After about three years, they swim to the ocean. They stay there for at least four years. Then, they return to rivers to lay their eggs.

FISH WITH MUSCLES
These fish are big and have large fins. They are strong enough to swim against the current of fast-flowing rivers.

UP RIVER

Pacific salmon migrate from the ocean in the autumn. After they have laid their eggs, they die. Atlantic salmon travel up river to lay eggs, then return to the sea.

A HARD JOURNEY

Salmon leap over waterfalls as they swim up river. Bears and otters hunt them.

A PLACE TO EAT

Salmon travel near the shore of rivers and streams. They find food in these shallow, calm places.

INDEX

GLOSSARY

Amphibian - An animal that lives partly on land and partly in water.

Bill - Another word for the beak of a bird.

Burrow - A tunnel or hole in the ground dug by an animal for its home.

Camouflage - Many animals blend with the color of the place where they live. This is called camouflage. Camouflage protects an animal from its enemies and hides it when it is trying to catch other animals.

Colony - A large group of animals living together is called a colony.

Den - The home or hiding place of a wild animal.

Lodge - A beaver's home is called a lodge. It is made of branches and sticks, and the inside and outside walls are covered with mud.

Migrate - When birds and animals migrate, they move to another place with the seasons.

Predator - The animal that hunts and kills other animals is called a predator.

Prey - An animal that is hunted is the prey.

Territory - An animal's territory is the area which it thinks of as its own.